How Baseball Managers Use Math

by John C. Bertoletti

Math Curriculum Consultant: Rhea A. Stewart, M.A.,
Specialist in Mathematics, Science,
and Technology Education

An Imprint of Chelsea House Publishers

Math in the Real World: How Baseball Managers Use Math

Copyright © 2010 by Infobase Publishing

Chelsea Clubhouse
An imprint of Chelsea House Publishers
132 West 31st Street
New York NY 10001

Library of Congress Cataloging-in-Publication Data
Bertoletti, John C.
        How baseball managers use math / by John C. Bertoletti; math curriculum consultant,
        Rhea A. Stewart.
            p. cm. — (Math in the real world)
        Includes index.
        ISBN 978-1-60413-604-3
        1. Mathematical statistics—Juvenile literature. 2. Mathematics—Juvenile literature.
        3. Baseball—Juvenile literature. I. Title. II. Series.
        QA276.13.B47 2010
        519.5—dc22   2009016265

Chelsea Clubhouse books are available at special discounts when purchased in bulk quantities for businesses, associations, institutions, or sales promotions. Please call our Special Sales Department in New York at (212) 967-8800 or (800) 322-8755.

You can find Chelsea Clubhouse on the World Wide Web at http://www.chelseahouse.com

Developed for Chelsea House by RJF Publishing LLC (www.RJFpublishing.com)
Text and cover design by Tammy West/Westgraphix LLC
Illustrations by Spectrum Creative Inc.
Photo research by Edward A. Thomas
Index by Nila Glikin

Photo Credits: 4, 14, 21, 23: Getty Images; 6: New York Post; 7, 8, 9, 10, 12, 16, 19, 24: AP/Wide World Photos; 17, 20, 22: MLB Photo via Getty Images; 18: © RICHARD CARSON/Reuters/Corbis; 26: TOM MAYES/CSM/Landov.

Cover printed by Bang Printing, Brainerd, MN
Book printed and bound by Bang Printing, Brainerd, MN
Date printed: October 2010
Printed and bound in the United States of America

10 9 8 7 6 5 4 3 2

Table of Contents

Answers and helpful hints for the You Do the Math
activities are in the Answer Key.

Words that are defined in the Glossary are
in **bold** type the first time they appear in the text.

Meet the Manager

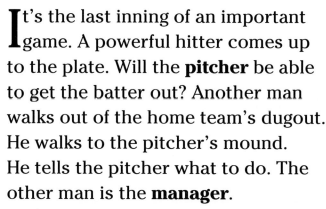

It's the last inning of an important game. A powerful hitter comes up to the plate. Will the **pitcher** be able to get the batter out? Another man walks out of the home team's dugout. He walks to the pitcher's mound. He tells the pitcher what to do. The other man is the **manager**.

A manager is the head coach of a baseball team. He decides which players play in games. He decides when to take a player out of a game. He studies information about the team his players are facing and uses that information to give his players instructions.

Manager Mike Scioscia (in red shirt) talks to his pitcher and catcher about how to pitch to the next batter.

Making Decisions

Managers are always making decisions, and they

often use math to do so. Managers rely on **data**, or information. The manager studies the data to make decisions about what his players should do.

The team will face pitcher Tim Monroe tonight. The manager wants to tell his players what kinds of pitches Monroe throws. If the batters know what kinds of pitches to expect, they are more likely to get hits.

The bar graph below shows the pitches Monroe threw in his last game. By reading the graph, the manager sees that Monroe threw mostly curve balls. Now the manager can tell his players that they will likely see a lot of curve balls from Monroe.

You Do the Math

Learn from the Data

Use the bar graph to answer these questions:

1. How many fastballs did Monroe throw?

2. How many fewer sliders than curve balls did he throw?

3. How many pitches did he throw all together?

4. Arrange the types of pitches in order, going from the type thrown most often to the type thrown least often.

Pitches Thrown by Tim Monroe

Number of Pitches Thrown — Type of Pitch Thrown

Decimals and Decision-Making

A manager makes many decisions. He decides which players will be in each game. He studies **statistics**. Statistics are data in number form. Some types of baseball statistics help managers know how players on their team are performing.

Batting average statistics tell managers how well each player is hitting the ball. A batting average is a decimal number in the thousandths place. A player's batting average is a number less than or equal to 1. In baseball, batting averages are written without the 0 in the ones place, like this: .267. (At other times, this number would be written 0.267.)

A player's batting average is calculated by taking the number of hits the player gets and dividing that by the number of times the player comes up to bat. The result is rounded to the nearest thousandth. Most baseball fans agree that an average of .300 or more is excellent.

Giants 1, Dodgers 0, 11 inn.

San Fran.	AB	R	H	BI	BB	SO	Avg
Winn lf	5	0	0	0	1	2	.308
Ochoa ss	3	0	0	0	0	1	.209
a-DRoberts ph	1	0	0	0	0	0	.214
Vizquel ss	0	0	0	0	1	0	.211
Schierholtz rf	5	0	0	0	0	1	.302
BMolina c	5	0	1	0	0	0	.292
Ishikawa 1b	4	0	1	0	0	1	.282
e-Bowker ph-1b	1	0	0	0	0	1	.247
Rowand cf	4	0	2	0	1	1	.276
McClain 3b	4	0	1	0	0	2	.310
f-Sandoval ph	1	0	0	0	0	0	.346
1-Hennessey pr	0	1	0	0	0	0	.286
Velez 2b	4	0	3	0	1	0	.256
Cain p	2	0	0	0	0	2	.117
Aurilia 1b-3b	2	0	1	1	0	0	.289
Totals	**41**	**1**	**9**	**1**	**4**	**11**	

Los Angeles	AB	R	H	BI	BB	SO	Avg
Martin c	4	0	1	0	1	1	.275
Ethier rf	5	0	2	0	0	1	.301
MRamirez lf	2	0	0	0	3	2	.399
Loney 1b	5	0	0	0	0	0	.291
Blake 3b	5	0	0	0	0	3	.245
Kemp cf	4	0	0	0	0	2	.289
Dewitt 2b	4	0	1	0	0	0	.260
Berroa ss	3	0	1	0	0	0	.238
c-DeYoung ph	1	0	0	0	0	0	.250
DLowe p	1	0	0	0	0	1	.141
b-Pierre ph	1	0	0	0	0	0	.271
d-MaSweeney ph	1	0	0	0	0	0	.135
Totals	**36**	**0**	**5**	**0**	**4**	**10**	

San Fran.	000	000	000	01	—	1	9	0
Los Angeles	000	000	000	00	—	0	5	0

This table, called a box score, from a newspaper shows the results of a baseball game. Each player's batting average is in the column on the far right.

A Way to Compare Players

A manager has to read and compare decimal numbers. Suppose a manager compares two players. He must decide which one will play in tonight's game. He reads their batting averages. Dave is hitting .309, and Matt is hitting .302. The manager compares these numbers. He reads them to the thousandths place. He knows 9 is greater than 2. That means .309 is a higher batting average than .302. The manager decides Dave will play.

Batter Cliff Floyd takes a big swing in a Major League Baseball game.

You Do the Math

Calculating Batting Averages

Calculate the batting averages for the players in the table below. Arrange the players in order of highest to lowest batting averages.

Players' Hits and Times at Bat		
Player	**Number of Hits**	**Number of Times at Bat**
Tom	30	120
Pedro	25	86
Alan	38	95
Felipe	35	150

A Night Game on the Road

A baseball team has a big game coming up. The manager wonders which players should play in the game. The game will be played at night. The game will be at the other team's stadium. (This is called an away game or a road game.) What does this have to do with decimal numbers? A lot.

The manager has statistics on all his players. By studying these statistics, he knows which ones play better in different situations. The manager compares decimal numbers to make decisions about which players will play in the big game.

Jacobs Field in Cleveland is all lit up for a night game.

Should Jaime Play?

Let's look at how Jaime Garcia is playing. Look at the data on page 9. In home games, Jaime's batting average is .311. In away games, it is .209.

Jaime hits .295 in day games. He hits .227 in night games. Should the manager let Jaime play?

Situation	Jaime's batting average
Home games	.311
Away games	.209

Situation	Jaime's batting average
Day games	.295
Night games	.227

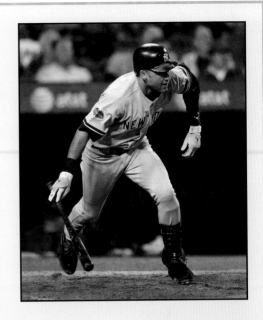

Derek Jeter runs to first base after getting a hit.

The manager knows .311 is a higher batting average than .209. Jaime hits better in home games. The manager knows .295 is higher than .227. Jaime hits better in day games.

The big game is at night and away. The manager will probably not play Jaime.

You Do the Math

Nighttime Batting Averages

The table below shows the batting averages in night games for four different players. Order the batting averages from least to greatest. Who has the highest night-game batting average? Who has the lowest?

Players' Night Game Batting Averages	
Player	**Game Batting Average**
Carlos Alvarez	.246
Elliot Davidson	.252
Marty Finnegan	.229
Josh Blackwell	.235

How's My Pitcher Doing?

The pitcher is the player who throws the ball to the batter. Managers can tell how well a pitcher is doing by looking at a type of statistic called the pitcher's **earned run average**. This is also called ERA for short.

ERA is the average number of runs a pitcher gives up in nine innings. ERA is a decimal number. To calculate ERA, take the number of **earned**

Johan Santana, pitching for the New York Mets, is about to throw a pitch in a game against the Chicago Cubs.

runs given up by the pitcher. Multiply that number by 9. Then, divide that by the number of innings the pitcher pitched.

Calculating Pete's ERA

Pete is a pitcher. In his last game, the other team scored 4 runs. Pete pitched 8 innings. Here is how Pete's ERA is calculated:

$$4 \times 9 = 36$$

$$36 \div 8 = 4.5$$

In baseball, ERA is written with two digits to the right of the decimal point. Pete's ERA for his last game is 4.50.

Good pitchers have low ERAs. Many baseball players and fans think a low ERA is 3.00 or less. Managers study their pitchers' ERAs very carefully to see how well each pitcher is doing.

You Do the Math

Which Pitcher Is Doing the Best?

Use the data in the table below to figure out which pitcher has the highest ERA. Who has the lowest ERA?

Pitchers' Runs Given Up and Innings Pitched		
Pitcher	Earned Runs Given Up	Innings Pitched
Don Smith	20	40
Willie Castillo	15	50
Bobby Mitchell	30	90

Is My Pitcher a Winner?

A manager and his pitcher have a quiet conversation in the dugout during a game.

Managers use ERA to analyze their pitchers. They also use the pitcher's **winning percentage**. The winning percentage is a statistic that tells the manager how many games the pitcher has won compared to how many games he has pitched.

After a game, one pitcher on the winning team is given credit for the win. Baseball fans say this pitcher "gets the win." One pitcher on the losing team "gets the loss." You get the win if you're the pitcher when your team takes the lead and keeps it for the rest of the game. You get the loss if you're the pitcher who gives up the winning run to the other team. Over the season, a pitcher has a record of wins and losses. A record of 7–4 means a pitcher has won 7 games and lost 4.

Finding the Winning Percentage

The manager uses a pitcher's record to calculate the pitcher's winning percentage. First, the manager looks at the total number of wins and losses the pitcher has. Then he sees how many games the pitcher has won. He divides the number of wins by the total number of wins and losses. For example, Tom has a record of 9 wins and 3 losses.

$$9 + 3 = 12$$

$$9 \div 12 = 0.75$$

In baseball, winning percentage is always written with three digits to the right of the decimal point and without the 0 in the ones place. Tom's winning percentage is .750. (This number can also be written as 75%.)

Here's another example. Jeff has a record of 12 wins and 8 losses. His winning percentage is .600:

$$12 + 8 = 20$$

$$12 \div 20 = 0.600$$

You Do the Math

How Did Juan Do This Season?

Juan has a record of 2 wins and 6 losses. What is Juan's winning percentage?

The Manager and His Percentages

The team has an important game on Friday. The team has two pitchers, Ruffino and Uribe, with excellent records. Who should pitch the game? The manager must decide.

First, the manager looks at both pitchers' records. Ruffino is 12–6. He's won 12 games. He's lost 6. Uribe is 6–2. He's won 6 games. He's lost 2.

Ruffino has won more games, but he also has pitched in more games. Which pitcher is doing better? It's hard to tell, so the manager calculates the winning percentages for both of them.

In this photo, Dusty Baker studies statistics when he was manager of the Chicago Cubs.

Ruffino or Uribe?

Here is how the manager calculates Ruffino's winning percentage:

$$12 + 6 = 18$$

$$12 \div 18 = 0.6666\ldots$$

Rounded to the nearest thousandth, this number becomes .667.

Next, the manager calculates Uribe's winning percentage:

$$6 + 2 = 8$$

$$6 \div 8 = 0.750$$

The manager sees that Ruffino's winning percentage is .667. That means that Ruffino has won almost 67% of his games. Uribe's winning percentage is .750. Uribe has won 75% of his games.

The manager knows that a higher percentage is better. He knows that 75% is greater than 67%. So Uribe seems to be pitching better. The manager makes his decision. Uribe will pitch on Friday.

You Do the Math

Which Team Is Having the Best Season?

Just as each pitcher has a won-lost record, the team as a whole has a won-lost record. So, just as you can calculate the winning percentage for a pitcher, you can also calculate the winning percentage for the team. The table below shows the wins and losses of four teams. Figure out the winning percentage of each team. Arrange the teams in order of highest winning percentage to lowest winning percentage. Which team is having the best season?

Four Teams' Wins and Losses		
Team	Number of Wins	Number of Losses
Skyhawks	48	34
Barons	52	30
Knights	42	40
Raptors	46	36

Why the Count Matters

Baseball managers sometimes explain key math ideas to their players to help them perform better. For example, managers explain how statistics relate to the **ball** and **strike count.**

Hideki Matsui waits for a pitch. For the pitch to be a strike, it must go over home plate no lower than his knees and no higher than halfway between his belt and his shoulders.

The count is how many balls and strikes a batter has. A strike is a pitch that goes in the **strike zone**. That means it goes over home plate at a level no lower than the batter's knees and no higher than halfway between the batter's shoulders and belt. A ball is a pitch thrown outside the strike zone. If the batter gets 3 strikes, he is out. If he gets 4 balls, he goes to first base. Balls are listed first in the count. Strikes are listed second. If the count is 2–1 ("two and one"), a batter has 2 balls and 1 strike.

Baseball statistics show that there is a connection between the count and a player's chances of reaching base safely. Suppose the count is 2–1. According to the data from years of baseball games, the batter has a good chance of reaching base. When the count is 0–2, he is less likely to get on base.

Improving Your Chances

Managers teach their players how to get the count in their favor. Suppose the count is 2–0. The batter has a good chance of reaching base. The manager explains that the batter should not swing at the next pitch if it looks like it will be a ball. A ball will make the count 3–0. At 3–0, the batter has an even better chance of reaching base. If he follows the manager's advice, the batter can increase his chances of getting on base.

The scoreboard at Comerica Park in Detroit shows how many balls and strikes the batter has.

You Do the Math

Figuring Out the Count

Here are some counts for you to figure out. How many balls and strikes are there in each count?

3–2   1–2   2–2   3–1

With which counts will the batter go to first base if he gets one more ball?

Intentional Walks

When a batter receives 4 balls and goes to first base, it is called a walk. Sometimes a manager gives instructions to his pitcher to walk the batter. This is called an **intentional walk**.

How does a manager decide if a batter should be walked? To do so, he uses probability. Probability is how likely it is that an event will happen. When thinking about probability, the manager uses words like *likely* and *unlikely* or *certain* and *impossible*. These words describe

When the catcher stands up and points his arm away from the batter, it is a signal to the pitcher that the manager wants to give the batter an intentional walk.

the chances that an event will occur. The manager must decide what will *most likely* happen if the batter is walked. The manager must also decide what will most likely happen if he isn't walked.

A manager, such as Joe Torre (left), will often talk about probability with his coaches.

Should We Walk Bill Walsh?

Bill Walsh comes up to bat. He is an excellent hitter. The manager thinks it is *likely* that Walsh will get a hit. He considers giving Walsh an intentional walk. The next batter will be Edgar Martinez. The manager knows that Martinez's batting average is much lower than Walsh's. Martinez is *unlikely* to get a hit.

What should the manager do? Walsh has a better chance of getting a hit than Martinez. The manager decides to walk Walsh. Probability helped the manager decide.

You Do the Math

Likely or Unlikely?

Think of a situation in a baseball game where the manager must use probability. Use words like *likely* and *unlikely* to describe the events.

Getting the Right Combination

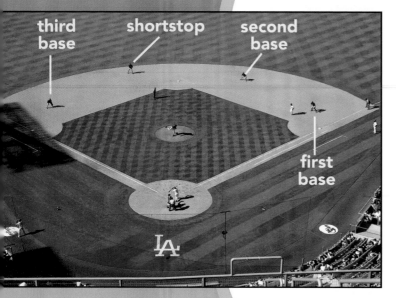

third base shortstop second base

first base

LA

This photo shows the infield at a Major League Baseball stadium. The labels name the positions played by the infielders.

A baseball team has two kinds of players. Some are pitchers. The rest are called position players. The position players include **catchers**, **infielders**, and **outfielders**. Catchers play behind home plate. They catch the pitches that are thrown by the pitcher and not hit by the batter. Infielders play in the infield. Outfielders play in the outfield (the part of the field beyond the infield).

The manager helps decide how many pitchers the team should have. He helps decide how many position players to have. He uses a number sentence:

Pitchers + Position Players = Total Number of Players

He could also use a different number sentence:

Total Number of Players − Pitchers = Position Players

Using the Number Sentence

A manager needs the right combination of players. He needs a mix of pitchers and position players. The

All of the players on the New York Mets line up before the start of a game.

total number of players on a Major League Baseball team is 25 for most of the season. Suppose a manager chooses to have 11 pitchers. How many position players will he have? Using the second number sentence:

$$25 - 11 = 14$$

The manager will have 14 position players.

Of course, the number of pitchers and position players must make baseball sense. Suppose there are only 4 pitchers. Each one would have to pitch a lot. They would get very tired. Soon, they would not be able to pitch as well. So the manager must make wise choices.

You Do the Math

Different Combinations

A team will have 14 position players. The manager wants 1 to 3 catchers. He wants 4 to 7 infielders. He wants 3 to 6 outfielders. Here is one combination he can have: 2 catchers, 6 infielders, and 6 outfielders. Write two other combinations a manager can have with these guidelines to make a team with 14 position players.

Should the Pitcher Bat?

Pitchers are often not very good hitters. In Major League Baseball, pitchers don't bat in American League games. In the National League, pitchers do bat. In a National League game, should the pitcher go up to bat when it's his turn to bat during a game? That's a decision a manager must make. This can be a tough choice. Fortunately, the manager understands probability. This helps him decide what to do.

The manager can take a pitcher out of the game before he bats. The manager can send in a **pinch hitter** for the pitcher. A pinch hitter bats in place of another player. When would a manager do this?

These two hitters are taking practice swings so that they will be ready if one of them is called into the game as a pinch hitter.

Using Probability to Decide

It's late in a game. The score is tied. The manager wants his team to get hits and score runs to take the lead.

The pitcher is due to bat next. The manager uses his knowledge of probability. He knows that the pitcher is not a good hitter, so the pitcher is *unlikely* to get a hit. The manager thinks about his pinch hitter. The pinch hitter has a good batting average. The manager decides the pinch hitter is *more likely* to get a hit than the pitcher.

The manager takes the pitcher out of the game. The pinch hitter bats instead and hits a home run! That's the winning run in the game. The manager's use of probability helped him make the right decision.

Pitcher Hiroki Kuroda waits to bat. Depending on the situation in the game, a manager may send a pinch hitter to bat in place of his pitcher.

You Do the Math

Making a Decision about Omar

Omar is a pitcher. He will bat next. His team is losing. He has been up to bat 20 times this year. He has 2 hits. If the manager takes Omar out of the game, a pinch hitter will hit. The pinch hitter has a batting average of .280. Should the manager let Omar bat? Or should he use a pinch hitter?

Keeping a Close Eye on the Pitch Count

It's the bottom of the 8th inning. The pitcher has been pitching the whole game. The manager wonders if the pitcher is tired. Maybe it is time to take him out of the game. The manager is not sure. Fortunately, there is an important statistic that helps him decide.

The **pitch count** is the number of pitches a pitcher has thrown in a game. A pitch count of 102 means the pitcher has thrown 102 pitches so far in the game. The more pitches a pitcher throws, the more tired he

When a manager wants to take his pitcher out of a game, he will come onto the field and take the ball from the pitcher.

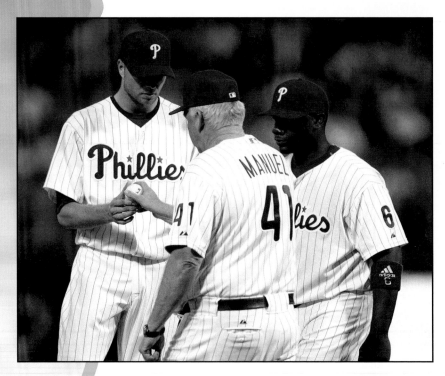

can get. The pitch count will help the manager decide about keeping the pitcher in the game.

Tired? You Probably Won't Pitch As Well

Baseball statistics show that pitchers start to pitch more poorly as they get tired. The more pitches a pitcher has thrown in a game, the more likely it is that the batter will get a hit. So managers have a decision to make when a pitcher's pitch count gets high. Most baseball experts agree that a high pitch count is around 100 or more. Many managers will take a pitcher out of a game before his pitch count gets much higher than 100.

Pitch Count and Wins

The table below shows data for one pitcher in the first five games he pitched in a new baseball season. Look at the data in the table. In which game did the pitcher have the highest pitch count? In which game did he have the lowest pitch count? What can you say about the relationship between the pitch count and the pitcher's wins?

Pitch Counts and Wins or Losses		
Date of Game	**Pitch Count**	**Won or lost**
April 10	90	won
April 16	105	lost
April 26	96	won
May 2	115	lost
May 7	118	lost

How to Choose a Relief Pitcher

Dan is a **starting pitcher**. A starting pitcher is the team's first pitcher in the game. He starts pitching at the beginning of the game. Dan just gave up a home run. The manager decides to take him out of the game.

A **relief pitcher** will come in. A relief pitcher comes in during a game to replace another pitcher.

The team has several relief pitchers. Who should pitch? The manager will choose either Paul or Scott. The manager will use data to help him make this decision.

Ken will bat next for the other team. The manager looks at Ken's statistics. He studies how Ken did when he batted against Paul and Scott in previous games. Then he does some calculations.

bullpen

Relief pitchers sit in an area called the bullpen, which is often in back of the outfield. This relief pitcher runs onto the field after being called into the game by his manager.

Batter and Relief Pitcher

Ken faced Paul 12 times. He got 3 hits. The manager divides:

$$3 \div 12 = 0.250$$

Ken has a .250 batting average when he bats against Paul.

The manager does the same thing for Scott. Ken faced Scott 18 times. He got 9 hits.

$$9 \div 18 = 0.500$$

Ken has a .500 batting average when he bats against Scott.

Ken's batting average was much lower against Paul than it was against Scott. The manager decides to bring Paul into the game to try to get Ken out. Paul is more likely to get Ken out than Scott is.

You Do the Math

Who Should Pitch Against Karl?

The manager must bring a new pitcher into the game to face Karl, a very good hitter. The table below shows how three different relief pitchers pitched against Karl in the past. Decide which of the three relief pitchers should come in to face Karl now.

Three Pitchers' Records Against Karl		
Pitcher	Number of Times He Faced Karl	Number of Hits He Gave Up
Oliver Martinez	16	12
Hal Church	24	12
Martin Smith	5	3

If You Want to Be a Baseball Manager

If you want to be a baseball manager, you must understand the game. Managers are considered baseball experts. They get that way by playing the game, so the first step to becoming a manager is to play baseball. Many managers were major league players. Many managers worked as coaches before they became managers. Coaches help a manager run the team.

Managers also study the game. They study the game's history. They learn all the rules. They understand the strategies. They understand the probabilities. Probabilities make some strategies good and other strategies bad.

What else will help someone become a good manager? Managers must understand people. A manager works with players all the time. He teaches them. He cheers them up when they are not playing well. He helps them play better.

And lastly, managers must be able to work with math! It helps them make the best decisions for their team.

Answer Key

Pages 4-5: Meet the Manager:
1. 35 fastballs. **2.** 40 (he threw 50 curve balls and 10 sliders; to find the difference, 50 − 10 = 40). **3.** 95 (35 + 50 + 10 = 95). **4.** curve balls, fastballs, sliders.

Pages 6-7: Decimals and Decision Making:
Alan .400, Pedro .291 (rounded from .2906…), Tom .250, Felipe .233 (rounded from .2333…).

Pages 8-9: A Night Game on the Road:
.229, .235, .246, .252. Elliot has the highest batting average. Marty has the lowest batting average.

Pages 10-11: How's My Pitcher Doing?:
Don has the highest ERA: 4.50. Willie has the lowest ERA: 2.70. Bobby's ERA is 3.00.

Pages 12-13: Is My Pitcher a Winner?:
Juan's winning percentage is .250, or 25%. 2 wins + 6 losses = 8 total wins and losses. 2 ÷ 8 = 0.250, or 25%.

Pages 14-15: The Manager and His Percentages:
Barons .634, Skyhawks .585, Raptors .561, Knights .512. The Barons are having the best season.

Pages 16-17: Why the Count Matters:
3–2: 3 balls and 2 strikes. 1–2: 1 ball and 2 strikes. 2–2: 2 balls and 2 strikes. 3–1: 3 balls and 1 strike. A batter with a 3–2 or 3–1 count will go to first base if he gets one more ball, for a total of 4.

Pages 18-19: Intentional Walks:
Sample answer: A batter with a low batting average is at bat. A great pitcher is pitching. The pitcher should not give the batter an intentional walk because the batter is unlikely to get a hit. The pitcher is likely to get the batter out.

Pages 20-21: Getting the Right Combination:
Sample answers: 3 catchers, 6 infielders, 5 outfielders; 2 catchers, 7 infielders, 5 outfielders.

Pages 22-23: Should the Pitcher Bat?
Sample answer: The manager should use a pinch hitter. Omar's batting average is only .100. The pinch hitter's batting average is .280, which is much higher. The pinch hitter is more likely to get a hit.

Pages 24-25: Keeping a Close Eye on the Pitch Count:
He had the highest pitch count on May 7. He had the lowest pitch count on April 10. Sample answer: The pitcher won games when his pitch count was low (under 100). He lost games when his pitch count was high (over 100).

Pages 26-27: How to Choose a Relief Pitcher:
Hal Church should pitch, because Karl has a .500 batting average against him. Karl has a .750 batting average against Oliver Martinez and a .600 batting average against Martin Smith. His batting average is lowest against Hal Church. Hal Church is more likely to get Karl out than either of the other two pitchers is.

Glossary

ball—A pitch that is thrown outside the **strike zone**.

batting average—A baseball statistic that tells how well a player is hitting.

catcher—A baseball player who catches the pitches thrown by the **pitcher**.

count—The number of **balls** and **strikes** a batter has when batting.

data—Information.

earned run—A run that the **pitcher** is responsible for having given up and that did not involve an error.

earned run average—A baseball statistic that tells the average number of runs a pitcher gives up in nine innings.

infielder—A baseball player who plays a position in the infield of the baseball field.

intentional walk—A walk that is given to a batter on purpose. Usually the **manager** tells the **pitcher** to give an intentional walk.

manager—The head coach of a baseball team.

outfielder—A baseball player who plays a position in the outfield of the baseball field.

pinch hitter—A baseball player who is brought into the game to bat for another player.

pitch count—The number of pitches a **pitcher** has thrown in one game.

pitcher—A baseball player who puts the ball into play by throwing it toward the batter.

relief pitcher—A **pitcher** who is brought into the game to replace another pitcher.

starting pitcher—A **pitcher** who starts pitching at the beginning of a game.

statistics—Data presented in the form of numbers.

strike—A pitch that is thrown inside the **strike zone**.

strike zone—Where a pitch must be thrown to be a **strike**. A pitch is in the strike zone if it goes over home plate at a height no lower than the batter's knees and no higher than halfway between the batter's shoulders and belt.

winning percentage—A baseball statistic that tells how often a pitcher has won games in which he has pitched.

To Learn More

Read these books:

Jennison, Christopher. *Baseball Math*. Tucson, Ariz.: Good Year Books, 2006.

McIntosh, Ned. *Managing Little League Baseball*. New York: McGraw-Hill, 2008.

Porterfield, Jason. *Baseball Rules, Tips, Strategy, and Safety*. New York: Rosen Publishing, 2007.

Thomas, Ron, and Joe Herran. *Getting into Baseball*. New York: Chelsea House, 2005.

Look up these Web sites:

About.com: Sports Careers
http://www.sportscareers.about.com/od/proteampositions/a/minorleague.htm

How to Become a Baseball Team Manager
http://www.ehow.com/how_2092263_become-baseball-team-manager.html

PowerPlayManager's Online Baseball Manager Game
http://www.baseball.powerplaymanager.com/en/online-baseball-manager-game.html

SimYard.Com's Strategic Baseball Manager
http://www.simyard.com

Key Internet search terms:

baseball, baseball manager, manager

Index

About the Author

John C. Bertoletti is a writer, educator, and lifelong Chicago White Sox fan. At a White Sox game in 1984, he jumped for joy after catching a foul ball off the bat of baseball Hall of Famer Reggie Jackson.